Precision, rather than self-expression, was the aim of art teaching, as it was with the teaching of writing. These two boys, at Llangadfan school, Powys, about 1910, are colouring identical pictures. The crispness of their collars contrasts with the muddiness of their boots. While the open door lets in light and air, the state of the floor shows that it also let in mud, clearly a great problem in rural areas.

THE
VICTORIAN SCHOOLROOM

Trevor May

Shire Publications Ltd

CONTENTS

Published in 1999 by Shire Publications Ltd, Cromwell House, Church Street, Princes Risborough, Buckinghamshire HP27 9AA, UK. Website: www.shirebooks.co.uk
Copyright © 1994 by Trevor May. First published 1994, reprinted 1995, 1996, 1998 and 1999. Shire Album 302. ISBN 0 7478 0243 2.
Trevor May is hereby identified as the author of this work in accordance with Section 77 of the Copyright, Designs and Patents Act 1988.

Printed in Great Britain by CIT Printing Services Ltd, Press Buildings, Merlins Bridge, Haverfordwest, Pembrokeshire SA61 1XF.

British Library Cataloguing in Publication Data: May, Trevor. Victorian Schoolroom. – (Shire Albums; No. 302). I. Title. II. Series. 371.00942. ISBN 0-7478-0243-2.

ACKNOWLEDGEMENTS
I would like to thank my wife, Jennifer, and my colleague and friend, Terry Prince, for their helpful suggestions. Illustrations are acknowledged as follows: Beamish, the North of England Open Air Museum, page 32; Durham County Records Office, page 5; Greater London Photographic Library, pages 3, 9, 13 (top); Harrow Local History Collection, Harrow Library Service, pages 2, 11 (top); Cadbury Lamb, pages 4 (bottom), 14 (top), 22 (bottom); Carol-Anne Lane, page 19; Macclesfield Museums Trust, page 4 (top); Manchester City Art Galleries, page 17; Pitstone Local History Society, page 14 (bottom); Radstock, Midsomer Norton and District Museum, page 24; Southwark Local History Library, page 6 (bottom); Welsh Folk Museum, pages 1, 16 (top); author, pages 6 (top), 8, 10, 11 (bottom), 12, 13 (bottom), 15, 16 (bottom), 20, 21, 22 (upper two), 23, 25, 26, 27.

The first elementary schools were often put up by the local builder and carpenter with no recourse to plans of any sort. However, once a government building grant became available, plans had to be submitted and approved. Very soon a distinctive school architecture began to emerge. Henry Kendall Jr was the son of one of the founders of the Royal Institute of British Architects. In 1847 he published a book of school plans, amongst which were those for Stanmore Infants School, Middlesex, which he had designed in 1845. This school, an example of those financed by a private patron, provided for one hundred children and cost £430, exclusive of site and internal fittings. This school continued in use until shortly before its demolition in the early 1960s.

An infant classroom in a London elementary school. Against a background of identical chalk-drawn swans is the day's lesson – on the duck! Notice the monogram of the London School Board cast in the desk supports.

THE ELEMENTARY SCHOOL

During the nineteenth century a system of education was founded in England and Wales under the direction of the central government. However, before 1902 the state provided only elementary education, which, to all intents and purposes, meant education for the working class. When Victoria came to the throne, some people still thought that the education of the poor was both unnecessary and dangerous. 'What produced the French Revolution?' asked one MP rhetorically, and the answer he gave was 'books'. Nevertheless, by the 1830s the fear of educating the poor had been surpassed by the greater fear of allowing them to remain ignorant, or of letting their education fall into dangerous hands. James Kay-Shuttleworth, an Assistant Poor Law Commissioner, and subsequently one of the great educational administrators, claimed in 1838 that the state had the responsibility 'of rearing ... children in religion and industry, and of imparting such an amount of secular education as may fit them to discharge the

duties of their station'. The aim, therefore, was to enforce social discipline and also to instill a new work discipline that would fit working-class children to the needs of an increasingly mechanical society.

Here was a great problem, however, for school competed with work for the child's time. This tension between sending children to work and sending them to school persisted throughout the nineteenth century. One solution was to make use of the one day in the week when the children's labour was not required – Sunday. For this reason, starting from the 1780s, children poured into Sunday schools, where they received training in basic literacy and numeracy as well as religious instruction. By 1851, well over two million working-class children were enrolled, while the Sunday School Union sold over ten million reading and spelling books in the first half of the nineteenth century. So widespread was the influence of Sunday schools that one historian has argued

Macclesfield Sunday School, soon after its opening in 1814. The external architecture is very similar to that of the mills which would have provided employment for many of the pupils.

The school building at New Lanark, completed in 1817. Some factory owners held a more enlightened view of education than others. In particular, Robert Owen held strong views on the importance of environment and children were treated with kindness at the elementary school he built at his New Lanark mills in Scotland. Twelve teachers were in charge of 194 children, a generous pupil-teacher ratio even by today's standards, and before he transferred it to the British and Foreign Schools Society in 1824 his school was a mecca for educational reformers.

4

GATESHEAD
BRITISH SCHOOL
FOR GIRLS,

In connection with the British School for Boys.

A School on the British or Lancasterian System will be opened for the Education of Girls on

MONDAY, THE 12th OF OCTOBER,

In the spacious SCHOOL ROOM under the

INDEPENDENT CHAPEL, MELBOURNE STREET.

The School will be conducted by MISS WRIGHT, from the British and Foreign School Society, Borough-road, London, of which Society, our gracious Sovereign the QUEEN, is a Patron, and a Subscriber of £100 per Annum ; the Lord Bishop of Norwich, and other Dignitaries of the Established Church, are also Patrons and Subscribers.

INHABITANTS OF GATESHEAD,

In this School your Children (above Six Years of Age) will receive a sound Scriptural Education. The Principles on which this School is founded enable it to admit the Children of Parents of every Religious Denomination, while it teaches the Doctrines of Religion from the Page of Divine Inspiration itself, (the introduction of the Sacred Scriptures, without Note or Comment, as the only Book of Religious Instruction, has been from the first a Fundamental Rule in all the Schools of the Society,) it excludes Creeds and Catechisms ; and thus, occupying the ground of our Common Christianity, it acts as a Powerful Auxiliary to Sabbath School Instruction, and leaves untouched the Formularies and Discipline of particular Churches.

The great object of the Promoters of these Schools being, that the Children may be Trained to Habits of Industry and Frugality in early life. the Girls will be allowed to bring with them their own Work to Make or Repair.

It is required, that the Girls come to School with their Hands and Faces Clean, their Hair Combed, and their Clothes Whole.

Instructions will be given in Reading, Writing, Arithmetic, Grammar, and Needle-Work.---Mothers will be allowed to send their elder Girls for *half a Day*, if more convenient.

Lectures on various Subjects will be given, during the Winter Evenings, to the Children of both the Schools.

TERMS.---2d. PER WEEK, TO BE PAID IN ADVANCE.
R. H. HAGGIE, Treasurer.

N.B. The British System has been long tried, both in this Country and in the British Colonies, and found to be one of the best Systems of Popular Instruction.

W. DOUGLAS, OBSERVER OFFICE, GATESHEAD.

Great play was made by the British and Foreign Schools Society that its schools gave a Christian but undemoninational education. This notice makes it clear that here, as elsewhere, cleanliness was considered next to godliness.

that they represented the 'single experience common to the children of an agricultural labourer in Bedfordshire, of a stockinger or handloom weaver in the Midlands, or of a factory operative in south Lancashire'.

In the eighteenth century great strides had been made in the provision of charity schools, where the children of the poor might be educated without having to pay fees. In Victorian times, also, voluntary effort to overcome social problems was the norm, and education was no exception. In 1808 the Royal Lancasterian Society was set up by the nonconformist supporters of Joseph Lancaster, and it was re-formed in 1814 as the British and Foreign Schools Society. Not to be outdone, the Church of England in 1811 formed the National Society for Promoting the Education of the Poor in the Principles of the Established Church. Other religious groups, notably the Wesleyans and the Roman Catholics, also established schools, but these two societies had the greater number. Both built schools throughout England, although the British and Foreign schools were confined largely to the towns, and there were far fewer of them. By the end of the 1850s there were

5

A Lancasterian model school, the Borough Road school of the British and Foreign Schools Society, at the beginning of the nineteenth century. The master stands on the extreme right. At the front of the school stands the 'monitor of order', whose task is to control the 360 or so boys in the school, who are here sitting at their writing desks. At the end of each row stands a 'monitor of class'. Each row, or class, is identified by a board placed on an upright standard, numbered from I to VIII. The term 'standard', which from 1862 became the universal name for a class, may derive partly from this practice. Around the walls are placed 'lessons' pasted to pieces of board, something like the hornbooks of an earlier period or the worksheets of our own day. Beneath the boards are wooden pointers which would be used by the monitors when giving their instruction. At such times the children being taught would stand at their 'draft station', a semicircle marked on the floor, facing the wall. The ceiling curtains are not for aesthetic effect, but to help deaden the noise that such large congregations of children created.

St Mary Newington School, Southwark, was built in 1820. This photograph of 1893 shows how conservative ideas about school layout could be, for the schoolroom is still arranged on lines that were set out by the Committee of Council in 1845. Although there are rows of desks running the length of the walls, the centre of the room is taken up with hollow squares typical of the monitorial method, as adopted by the National Society. The school was not demolished until 1966.

seventeen times as many National schools as there were British and Foreign. Most of the country had voluntary schools of one description or another, and hundreds of their former buildings are still in regular use today.

Lancaster and Andrew Bell, the champion of the Anglicans, each claimed to have invented the *monitorial system* of education. However, the system predates both men, and the significance of their rival claims is that it reflects the strong denominational rivalry that was to bedevil the provision of elementary schools.

The monitorial system was ideally suited to the new industrial age, for one of the principles upon which it was founded was the division of labour. Bell said of the system that 'like the steam engine, or spinning machinery, it diminishes labour and multiplies work', an apt simile for a very mechanical method of teaching. The aim, as in any factory, was to economise on the most expensive resource, in this case the teacher. The solution was for the teacher to instruct some of the older children, who then had the task of passing on this instruction to others. As a result it was claimed that one master or mistress could, if necessary, assume responsibility for the instruction of several hundred children at one time.

The monitorial system is now generally derided, but it did help to meet an urgent need for basic education. Its main drawback was the sterile rote-learning that was

7

An idealised view of a school playground in the 1870s. The accompanying text notes that 'neither managers nor teachers like the trouble of exercising supervision over the pupils during the hours of play ... the consequence is, that a spirit of lawlessness often reigns supreme in the playground ... and the more timid children are kept in a state of terror.' (From E. R. Robson, 'School Architecture', 1874.)

an inevitable outcome, while the noise in the schoolroom must, at times, have been unbearable. For this reason, Lancaster recommended that the schoolroom should have no ceiling, for that would act as a sounding board, and suggested that the floor be made of rammed clay or hard brick rather than more resonant timber or flagstones.

The monitorial system had a great impact on the layout of the schoolroom. The National Society reported in 1816 that 'a barn furnishes no bad model, and a good one may be easily converted into a school'. This description was repeated in the first government building regulations, issued in 1840. The oblong shape of early nineteenth-century schoolrooms was still being advocated in the building regulations of 1870-1, although by that date class teaching had come into more regular use.

English education offers many examples of new practice spreading outwards from the infant school. One such was the separate classroom, where a small group of children is taught directly by the teacher. Pioneering work in infant education was carried out by Samuel Wilderspin, who opened a model school at Spitalfields in London in 1820. Similar work was being done in Scotland (whence came much that was best in British education) by David Stow. Wilderspin and Stow emphasised the importance of physical activity, and pioneered the provision of well-equipped playgrounds. They also recommended the use of tiered seating or 'galleries'. Lancaster had earlier advocated a sloping floor, in order that the teacher could see the children. The infant pioneers were more concerned that the children should see the teacher. Galleries could be built in the oblong schoolroom, but Wilderspin stressed the provision of a small 'class room' in which the master or mistress could engage in the direct teaching of classes of children in turn, while monitors supervised the rest of the chil-

A drill lesson in a London school. There is no lawlessness here. Great stress was placed on drill at the end of the nineteenth century to combat the physical deterioration which was felt to be a consequence of urban living.

dren. However, an extended use of physically separate classrooms was dependent on a greater supply of teachers and that was not to come until after 1846.

At first, the voluntary schools were self-financing, but in 1833 the government voted a building grant of £20,000. However, sums would only be paid when at least half the cost of school buildings had been raised by private subscription. This was a serious shortcoming, for the poorest areas, where needs were greatest, were least able to put up their share. There were initially no approved designs for buildings, and no provision for ensuring maintenance or efficient instruction once a school was built. The grant was nevertheless renewed annually until 1838, but in the following year the government attempted to go further. A new Committee

of Council was established to oversee elementary education; a body of Her Majesty's Inspectors was appointed; and grant aid was placed on a more regular footing.

Through its Minutes, the Committee of Council was now able to lay down what were, in effect, building regulations. The first, issued in 1840, attempted to steer a course between traditional practice and more advanced thinking over such questions as the merits of monitorial ('mutual') methods and class teaching by the master or mistress (the 'simultaneous method'). The plans which were published implied a mixture of the two. Pupils' desks were placed on steps, somewhat shallower than those in an infants' gallery, so that the master might, from time to time, give a simultaneous lesson to the whole school. In larger schools provision was made for

9

SIDE ELEVATION

FRONT ELEVATION

SECTION

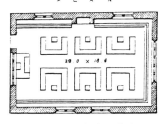

LOBBY · CLOSET · LOBBY

Plans for a school for 56 children (incorporating a house for the master) published by the Committee of Council on Education in 1840. These plans reflect the attempt made by the central government to adopt a neutral position with regard to the preferences of the principal voluntary societies. Thus, while suggesting its own layout of the schoolroom, the Committee added alternative plans adapted to the practice of the National and British and Foreign Schools Societies. In their own plan, the master's seat faces the children, who are arranged in four rows of tiered desks. The block of desks is centrally divided by a movable wooden partition, so that boys and girls might, if desired, be kept separate. The Committee did not advocate such a division, preferring instead the Scottish model where boys and girls sat on alternate benches according to their proficiency in the Three Rs. Placing the children's desks along the length of the schoolroom in this manner allowed the master either to teach the whole school simultaneously or to call out one class at a time to stand around his desk while the other classes (which remained under his watchful eye) could be taken by monitors.

PLAN

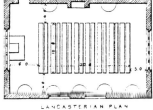

NATIONAL SCHOOL PLAN

LANCASTERIAN PLAN

the partial partitioning of the schoolroom into separate 'classrooms', while still allowing the master to keep an eye on the monitors elsewhere in the room. Minimum floor areas were laid down, fluctuating between 6 and 10 square feet (0.6 to 0.9 square metres) per child up to the 1860s in comparison with the 19 to 33

The interior of Greenhill Boys' School, a building erected by the Harrow School Board in 1896 to replace an earlier National school of 1859. The schoolroom retains the drawn-out oblong shape, although sliding partitions enable the room to be divided into three separate classrooms.

(Left) Although the school boards set out to erect permanent buildings (or to take over such buildings from the voluntary societies), the demand for elementary education was such that temporary buildings sometimes had to be resorted to. About 1900 William Cooper, a London manufacturer, advertised a 40 foot by 30 foot (12 by 9 metres) iron school for £155, erected complete. As late as 1899, London had 23 schools housed in 62 iron buildings and providing eight thousand places. The 'portable school' shown here is from an earlier decade and was featured in 'The Illustrated London News' in January 1857. The wooden building cost £60 and was designed to accommodate one hundred children, 'where a site or funds are difficult to obtain, or where the ground is undermined, or the population fluctuating'.

square feet (1.8 to 3.1 square metres) per child (dependent on age) required for primary schools in the 1990s.

It became clear to many people that the government would have to do more than subsidise voluntary effort if the needs of the whole country were to be met, for there were many places where the supply

11

The first elementary school to be built in the 'Queen Anne' style was Harwood Road School, Fulham, designed for the London School Board in 1873 by the eminent architect Basil Champneys. The half-acre (0.2 hectare) site cost £1,600, and the building (exclusive of furniture) cost £5,716. This worked out at just over £10 per head for the 727 children it was intended to serve. E. R. Robson, from whose book, 'School Architecture', the illustration is taken, described the building as 'a quaint and able adaptation of old English brick architecture to modern school purposes'.

of schools remained inadequate. However, the direct provision of schools by the state posed political problems, not the least of which was a denominational controversy over the place of religion in state schools.

Not until 1870 was a way forward established, when the Education Act of that year provided for the setting up of publicly elected school boards wherever voluntary provision was inadequate. The intention was not to replace the voluntary schools but to fill the gaps. However, rate-aid to the school boards (which did not have to balance their financial demands against other local needs) meant that the schools of the new local authorities could be built on a scale and to a standard which the voluntary societies found difficult to match.

Critics argued that board schools were too lavishly appointed. It was observed in 1887, for example, that the estimated cost of such schools was £12 9s 10d per child, compared with £5 7s 0d for new voluntary schools. However, these figures included the cost of land, which was often given by a benefactor for a voluntary school. In urban areas, where land costs were high, it was frequently found desirable to build elementary schools several storeys high, and schools for 1500 children soon became commonplace. Sir Arthur Conan Doyle had his character Sherlock Holmes liken the London board schools to lighthouses – 'Beacons of the future!' Many of them were both massive and grand. The London School Board had E. R. Robson as its architect between 1871 and 1889, and he developed a distinctive architectural style, 'Queen Anne', in reaction against the Gothic style which had previously been the fashion.

Large schools posed particular problems of health and hygiene, and questions of sanitation and ventilation were much debated. The development of a style in which classrooms opened on to a central hall provided what one architect called 'a magazine for air' and also facilitated movement around the school. George Widdows, county architect of Derbyshire, thought that there were other motives for

A game of skittles introduces children to numbers at Southfields Infants' School, London, in 1908. The essential features of the 'central hall' design are clear. From the hall the head teacher can clearly see what is going on in any of the adjoining classrooms. The equipment in the hall is typical and includes a piano and a display cabinet for trophies or for the 'school museum'. There is also a maypole and a rocking horse, use of the latter, no doubt, being a reward for good work. The Union Jack is a potent imperial symbol, while portraits of the King and Queen hang beside a print of Holman Hunt's painting, 'The Light of the World' – a Christian, though undenominational icon.

Brook Street Ragged School, near Euston Station (from 'The Illustrated London News', 17th December 1853). Some children, including many orphans, were utterly destitute and were quite unable the pay the 'school pence' demanded by voluntary schools. The pioneer of their education was John Pounds, a Portsmouth cobbler who opened a school in his workshop in 1818. Lord Shaftesbury became the patron of ragged schools, and a Ragged School Union was founded in 1844. At the peak of the movement, in the late 1860s, there were over six hundred such schools, more or less equally divided between day, evening and Sunday schools. The ragged school movement provides another example of the philanthropic provision of elementary education in the Victorian period.

the central hall design. It had been developed, he said, 'with the idea of giving the head teacher very little walking exercise. By seating him at a lordly desk, and by providing spy holes called borrowed lights, the head teacher was converted into a kind of glorified policeman, instead of being, as he should, a guide, philosopher and friend of children and teachers.'

The chalk circle on the floor of this reconstructed schoolroom of 1845 at the Ulster-American Folk Park, County Tyrone, Northern Ireland, marks the position to be taken by pupils as they worked under the instruction of a monitor. These 'draft stations' can also be seen in the picture of Borough Road school on pages 6-7. Irish schools (like those in Scotland) were administered separately from those in England, while schools in Wales came under a separate Welsh Department in 1907.

Children at Long Marston in Hertfordshire celebrate May Day. After 1903 this festival was followed by Empire Day, held on 24th May, the anniversary of Queen Victoria's birth.

Thomas Bewick, perhaps England's finest wood engraver, was much respected by the Romantics. Indeed William Wordsworth wrote, 'O that the genius of Bewick were mine.' This engraving, produced in the period just before Queen Victoria's accession, presents a romantic image of school, contrasting with Bewick's own schooldays, when he frequently played truant because of bullying. The dress of the adults (particularly the woman's bonnet) would suggest that they are visitors rather than the regular teachers.

THE SCHOOL TEACHER

The status of 'teachers' varies enormously, even in the present day. University lecturers, public-school masters, secondary-school subject specialists and infant teachers are likely to be perceived by society in very different ways. Such teachers may also be members of different trade unions or professional associations. These distinctions were even more sharply recognised in the nineteenth century.

Public-school masters enjoyed the status of gentlemen, although this was derived as much from their frequently being clergymen as from their being teachers of the young. The status of elementary-school teachers was in marked contrast. Those who taught working-class children were themselves drawn from the ranks of the working class. The concern that the poor should not be educated above their station led to a belief that teachers, too, should remain appropriately humble. This view dominated teacher training for much of the nineteenth century. What middle-class providers of education for the poor did not look for in a teacher was any real spirit of independence. It was largely for this reason that dame schools and common day schools were so widely condemned. Such schools were provided by working people for themselves and represent a remarkably widespread and persistent example of working-class 'private school education'. It is only in recent years that historians have probed beyond the derogatory comments in government reports and have come to see why working people appreciated for so long these schools of their own. The proprietors of such schools were officially condemned

The dame's school, or common day school, has, until recently, been much derided. Such schools certainly contrasted with the attempts at ordered efficiency made by the schools provided by voluntary societies and school boards. The official view of common day schools sometimes bordered on caricature, as does the illustration below taken from George C. T. Bartley, 'The Schools for the People', 1871. The photograph above is of Roath village school, near Cardiff, and was taken in 1899. Although conditions in these two schools are cramped, the possibility of movement is suggested. Their informality, their similarities to the homes from which the children came and the greater control which parents could exercise over the teachers were amongst the reasons why so many working people continued to patronise such schools, despite the opposition of the authorities.

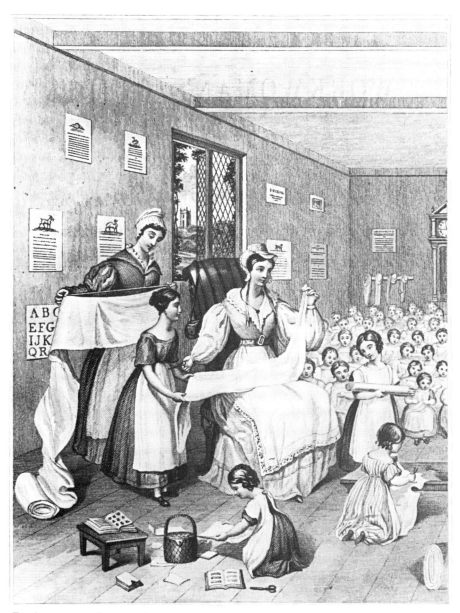

Teachers, especially in rural schools, were never free from visitors who might wish, at any time, to take over their class. Religion was often taught by the local clergyman, whose daughters might condescend to teach sewing to the girls. The ability to do plain sewing was as useful to the future domestic servant as it was to the future labourer's wife. (From 'The Workwoman's Guide', by 'A Lady', 1838.)

17

for their lack of training, but in the early nineteenth century most teachers even in the schools of the voluntary societies were largely untrained. Only with an increased supply of trained teachers could the monitorial system be replaced, and separate classrooms become more normal. The first moves in this direction came in 1846.

An unsuccessful attempt to introduce state-aided training colleges had been made in 1839 but had been dropped because of religious opposition. The voluntary societies were obliged to take action themselves. By 1845 the Church of England had opened twenty-two colleges (with places for 540 students) and by 1868 there were thirty voluntary colleges in England. Funding them was a major task for, while benefactors might support a local school, it was much more difficult to raise funds for a college which did not carry such immediately local benefits. In 1846, therefore, the government adopted new Minutes which passed most of the cost of training teachers on to the state, although the colleges remained denominational.

The pupil-teacher system which was adopted was, in effect, a form of apprenticeship. In schools approved by one of Her Majesty's Inspectors, children of thirteen could be apprenticed to a teacher for five years. Guided by the teacher, they were to do some of the teaching in school and were to receive additional instruction themselves. If, at the end of each year, their work proved satisfactory when examined by an HMI, both pupil teacher and school teacher received a government grant. At the end of their apprenticeship, pupil teachers presented themselves for the Queen's Scholarship examination, which allowed the most able of them to attend training college for three years. Those who were unsuccessful in securing a place, but whose work was of a certain standard, were awarded a Certificate of Merit which carried with it an annual grant towards their salaries. For the five years of their training in school, pupil teachers received a government grant ranging from £10 a year for those in their first year to £20 for those in their fifth. In many small rural schools, the head teachers had such

limited academic qualification that they were not deemed suitable to teach an apprentice. In their situation, or where the school itself lacked facilities, the post of stipendiary monitor was created. In this way, young people between the ages of thirteen and seventeen might be appointed as cheap substitutes for pupil teachers, earning for themselves an annual stipend of between £5 and £12 10s during the four years of their employment.

The regime of training colleges remained harsh throughout the century. So that they would not forget their social origins or the rank of those they were about to teach, students were required to undertake much manual labour. At Culham College in Oxfordshire, duties included 'sweeping rooms, fire-lighting, corridor cleaning, garden, postman, chapel cleaning, and town messenger'. Diet was frugal, and there were few facilities for recreation. When the provision of a common room was mooted at Lincoln in 1896, the college magazine expressed the hope 'that the Recreation Room, which is one of the latest fads, may not, with its lounges and luxurious easy chairs convert steady, working, industrious girls into mere imitations of fine ladies'.

The curriculum of the training colleges was both narrow and shallow. James Runciman, a student at Borough Road College in 1871-2, was shocked to find 'that he was expected to learn his country's story from a tiny fivepenny book, which contained strings of dates and names arranged in horrifying sequence'. It is not surprising, therefore, that lessons in elementary schools were frequently tedious and lacking in intellectual demand. While history consisted largely of learning strings of dates, geography was characterised as 'capes and bays', where children were required to learn such useless facts (because they were learnt in complete isolation) as the sequence of places around a coastline.

The work of teachers was mechanical, and they were paid a mechanic's wage for doing it. Salaries ranged widely. A teacher in a board school might earn twice as much as one in a church school, while men invariably earned more than women. In London, £60 to £150 was the scale for male assistants in the 1880s. In contrast, one village school offered the mistress £16 with house and garden, with work for her husband on the farm.

IN NATVRE'S INFINITE BOOK
OF SECRECY
A LITTLE CAN I READ

THE COMMITTEE OF HER MAJESTY'S MOST HONOURABLE PRIVY COUNCIL ON EDUCATION,
DEPARTMENT OF SCIENCE AND ART.
LONDON, S.W.

I*T is hereby Certified that* Jane Woodth......

obtained a First Class in the Elementary Stage of Physiography, at the Examination held on the 12th May, 1890.

BY ORDER,

N.B.—At this Examination 14,972 Candidates presented themselves. Of these, 205 came up in Honours, 2,522 in the Advanced Stage, 12,243 in the Elementary Stage. The results were as follows:—In Honours, 4 obtained a First Class, 20 a Second Class, and 181 failed. In the Advanced Stage, 334 obtained a First Class, 1,403 a Second Class, and 789 failed. In the Elementary Stage, 3,840 obtained a First Class, 6,352 a Second Class, and 2,049 failed.

Teachers could increase their qualifications and their salary by taking the examinations of the Science and Art Department, established in 1856 and merged into the Board of Education in 1899. If nothing else, the certificate was markedly more impressive than the ordinary Teachers' Certificate.

19

Words of two syllables accented on the first.

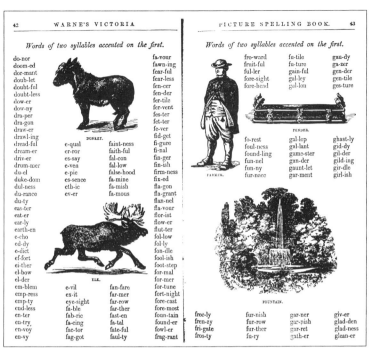

do-nor	e-qual	faint-ness	fa-vour
doom-ed	er-ror	faith-ful	fawn-ing
dor-mant	es-say	fal-con	fear-ful
doub-let	e-ven	fal-low	fear-less
doubt-ful	e-pic	false-hood	fen-cer
doubt-less	es-sence	fa-mine	fen-der
dow-er	eth-ic	fa-mish	fer-tile
dow-ny	ev-er	fa-mous	fer-vent
dra-per			fes-ter
dra-gon	DONKEY.		fet-ter
draw-er			fe-ver
drawl-ing			fid-get
dread-ful			fi-gure
dream-er			fi-nal
driv-er			fin-ger
drum-mer			fin-ish
du-el			firm-ness
duke-dom			fix-ed
dul-ness			fla-gon
du-rance			fla-grant
du-ty			flan-nel
eas-ter			fla-vour
eat-er			flor-ist
ear-ly			flow-er
earth-en			flut-ter
e-cho			fol-low
ed-dy			fol-ly
e-dict			fon-dle
ef-fort			fool-ish
ei-ther			foot-step
el-bow			for-mal
el-der	ELK.		for-mer
em-blem	e-vil	fan-fare	for-tune
emp-ress	ex-it	far-mer	fort-night
emp-ty	eye-sight	far-row	fore-cast
end-less	fa-ble	far-ther	fore-most
en-ter	fab-ric	fast-en	foun-tain
en-try	fa-cing	fa-tal	found-er
en-voy	fac-tor	fate-ful	fowl-er
en-vy	fag-got	faul-ty	frag-rant
free-ly	fren-zy	fri-gate	fros-ty

Words of two syllables accented on the first.

fro-ward	fu-tile	gau-dy	
fruit-ful	fu-ture	ga-zer	
ful-ler	gain-ful	gen-der	
fore-sight	gal-ley	gen-tile	
fore-head	gal-lon	ges-ture	
FENDER.			
fo-rest	gal-lop	ghast-ly	
foul-ness	gal-lant	gid-dy	
found-ling	game-ster	gil-der	
fun-nel	gan-der	gild-ing	
fun-ny	gaunt-let	gir-dle	
fur-nace	gar-ment	girl-ish	
FARMER.			
FOUNTAIN.			
fur-nish	gar-ner	giv-er	
fur-row	gar-nish	glad-den	
fur-ther	gar-ret	glad-ness	
fu-ry	gath-er	glean-er	

Despite its title, 'The Victoria Picture Spelling Book', published in 1872 at a price of one shilling, was intended to provide material for the whole curriculum, including not only reading, writing and arithmetic ('the Three Rs'), but history and geography. A book such as this, 152 pages in length, could well be the only reading matter that an elementary school child would encounter in the course of a year.

THE SCHOOL DAY

The school day for much of the Victorian period lasted six hours. The morning session generally ran from 9 a.m. to 12 noon, when there was a break of two hours, necessary because most children had to walk back to their homes for a meal. The afternoon session commenced at 2 p.m. and ran until 5 p.m., although some schools finished an hour earlier in the winter months, and from the 1880s onwards the length of the day had generally been reduced by half an hour. The length of lessons varied, although there was some appreciation of the fact that the attention span of young children was very limited. The Code of 1891 gave specific advice on the length of lessons for infants:

'It is essential ... that the length of the lesson should not ... exceed thirty minutes, and should be confined in most cases to twenty minutes; and that the lessons should be varied in length according to the section of the school, so that in the babies' room the actual work of the lessons should not be more than a quarter of an hour.'

Some idea of the allocation of time between subjects can be deduced from the curriculum of the Clifton Road Boys' School, Norwood, in 1886. Out of a school week totalling 27 hours and 30 minutes, 2 hours and 50 minutes were devoted to prayers and scripture. Depending on the class, between 3 hours and 20 minutes and 4 hours and 40 minutes was devoted to reading. Arithmetic accounted for be-

Reading was taught using wall charts such as this one (actual size: 41 by 30 inches, or 104 by 75 cm) dating from about 1900. The perceived need to start with single-syllable words before proceeding to words of two or more syllables could result in sentences that were more or less nonsensical.

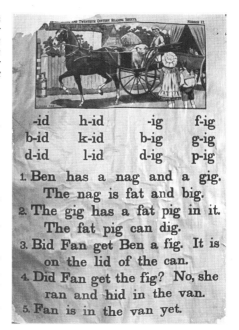

tween 3 hours and 45 minutes and 5 hours and 5 minutes (plus a further 1 hour and 10 minutes on mental arithmetic throughout the school). Between 3 hours and 45 minutes and 4 hours and 30 minutes was spent on spelling and dictation.

One day was very much like another, although some lessons appeared on the timetable only once a week, such as singing or the 'object lesson'. The latter had its origin in the view of some educationists, such as Heinrich Pestalozzi (1746-1827), that children learn through their senses, and should be led from the known to the unknown, and from the concrete to the abstract.

The method was considered particularly suitable for teaching science, and consisted of bringing into the classroom either natural or man-made objects, each of which would form the basis of a lesson. The principles were brought out clearly by James Currie in his *Common School Education*, a popular training manual for teachers towards the end of the nineteenth century:

'The object should be exhibited, if it be a substance (such as glass or sugar), for the inspection of the class; and the qualities important to be noticed should be observed by the appropriate senses. The action of the several senses is not to be

CABINETS OF ACTUAL OBJECTS FOR OBJECT LESSONS.

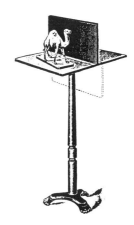

Cox & Company of London advertised their cabinets of specimens for object lessons in 1902 at about the same time as the Educational Supply Association was offering an object lesson stand.

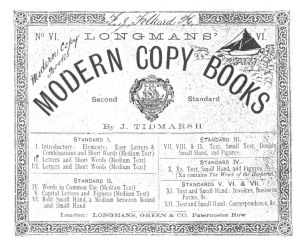

A copy book of the 1880s. The urge to embellish the covers of exercise books is a universal one! This book belonged to PC Frederick James Folkard, a Beccles policeman, who started on it in April 1886. Many children left school deficient in basic skills, and it was not uncommon for them to try to catch up in adult life.

The school signal was a device used in Victorian and Edwardian schools for securing attention. The sharp clicking sound that was produced could be used to send coded messages to the children, and the signals were produced in different sizes. That designed for head teachers had a more pronounced click.

interchanged: thus a quality cognizable by touch alone, such as hardness, is not to be vouched for by the sight, but verified by the sense of touch. The actual inspection of the aggregate of the qualities must be so distributed over the class, that as little shall be taken by them on trust as possible.'

The educational principles were sound enough. In practice, object lessons frequently degenerated into boring rote learning; while the lists of such lessons given throughout the term (often to be found in school log books) indicate that there was rarely any coherent relationship between one session and the next.

An exodus of farm labourers to the towns, especially in the later nineteenth century, meant that many rural schools could fulfil their function over a long period without need of extension. Willen School, in Buckinghamshire, was built in 1847 to accommodate thirty children, but in 1907 the average attendance was only twenty-four. Punctuality was one of the 'Victorian values' that schools attempted to instil, making the school bell an essential piece of equipment.

EQUIPPING THE SCHOOLROOM

One of the most marked contrasts between the nineteenth-century schoolroom and those of the present day lies in the range and quality of furniture and equipment. The bareness of Victorian schoolrooms is a striking feature of contemporary pictures and comes through clearly in documentary sources. In 1860, for example, the Assistant Secretary of the Education Department described the elementary schools of the early nineteenth century as having 'no furniture but a teacher's desk, a few rickety forms, a rod, a cane, and a fool's cap'.

The managers of voluntary schools were often reluctant to spend money on equipment of any sort. How little a school might contain is suggested by the valuation of Garth School, for 240 boys and girls, which was taken over by the Bangor School Board in 1875. The furniture was valued as follows:

In the boys' school: 12 parallel desks with forms in large room; 1 large cupboard and platform, 5 small cupboards, 1 large bell.

In the girls' school: 12 parallel desks with forms and stationery; platform filled with cupboards and drawers; 1 moveable desk and forms.

Value in all £21 9s 6d.

Early schoolrooms were simply shells for teaching, with seating the only requirement and even then not for all the pupils at one time. At first, benches were commonly used. Matthew Arnold HMI was still complaining of loose benches in 1872, believing them to encourage 'inattentiveness and lounging', but by then the desk had come into general use.

The iron-framed school desk, with its seat and top cut from solid oak, proved the most enduring of items, and many had a working life of eighty years or more. The introduction of the School Boards after 1870 meant that many authorities established central purchasing departments, and the placing of large orders gave a great fillip to a specialised branch of the furniture industry. Many desks were designed to be convertible, a practice which found no favour with J. G. Fitch HMI. He wrote in 1881: 'I would have you distrust all contrivances by which desks ... undertake to serve two purposes, e.g. to turn over and furnish a back suited for older people in a lecture-room, or to be fixed horizontally two together to make a tea-table.' That such desks were frequently advertised and appear to have been

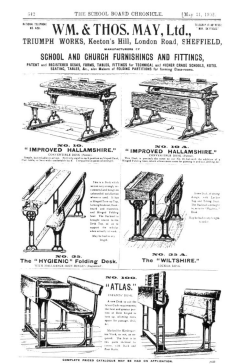

It was through advertisements in such journals as 'The School Board Chronicle' that manufacturers hoped to tap into the larger markets for equipment that were opened up by the school boards. Most manufacturers provided a number of different models of desk, each with its own name. Those shown here were advertised in May 1902.

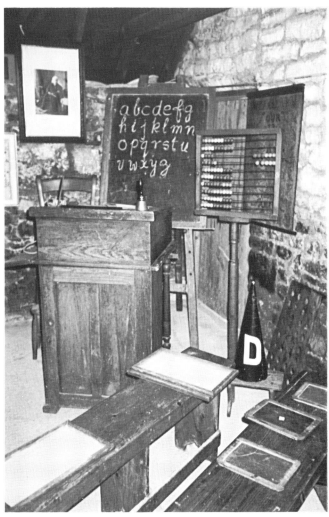

A reconstructed schoolroom at Radstock, Midsomer Norton and District Museum in Avon. On the front row of desks can be seen two sand trays, used to teach children their letters and numbers. Cheapness was the attraction of this piece of equipment, but some modern educationists see value in sand trays, with which young children can 'feel' the marks that they are making.

popular reflects the fact that many schoolrooms were expected to serve other purposes, such as a general meeting-hall for the community.

In classroom teaching the blackboard came to be the principal teaching aid with the result that 'chalk and talk' became a standard description of formal teaching methods. Free-standing boards were considered preferable to those attached to walls and were either set on easels or hung on pivoted frames.

Illustrations of Victorian schoolrooms often show the walls to have been bare, especially in the early part of the century. If anything was displayed in the early voluntary schools it was as likely as not to be some sort of 'improving' text. Some blood-curdling examples could be found: those in one infant school included the warning that 'All liars shall have their part in the lake that burneth with fire and brimstone'. By the end of the century, photographs show classrooms with a few

framed pictures or maps, as well as examples of children's work, but most artwork exhibited a dreary uniformity, in which self-expression found no place.

The provision of cheap yet appropriate reading matter was a major concern. Writing materials were less of a problem, partly because sand trays and slates were widely employed, thus reducing to a minimum the amount of paper that had to be purchased. Writing in ink in a copy book was reserved for older children, and to 'blot one's copy book' was a great crime. Copying was the norm. Professor H. C. Dent had been a pupil in an elementary school in 1904. He later wrote: 'I wrote endlessly, in "copy-books", morally elevating maxims, "A stitch in time saves nine", "Too many cooks spoil the broth" – but I never composed, much less wrote, in class a single original sentence.'

The importance attached to moral training had meant that the Bible was the principal reading book in most schools until about 1850, at which time Her Majesty's Inspectors came increasingly to oppose the practice. Apart from the technical problems of language, it was argued that the use of Bibles as reading books caused them to become tattered, with the result that children treated the scriptures with

little reverence. In addition it was feared that they would associate their reading difficulties with religion itself. To school managers, however, the Bible remained an attractive choice. With generous discounts from the Society for Promoting Christian Knowledge, a New Testament could be obtained in 1847 for 6d, whereas the fourth reader (a secular book) cost 1s 6d.

Reading books became available in greater quantities from the 1850s, although it is questionable whether their quality improved. Too often they consisted of the work of hack writers, and little attempt was made to introduce children to great works of literature. The Revised Code had a restrictive effect on book publishing: publishers proudly proclaimed that their minimal offerings provided all that was necessary to satisfy the law.

The Education Act of 1870 led to a vast expansion in the production of schoolbooks, which also came to reflect the more liberal curriculum of the later years of the century. Collins, for example, listed over a thousand school books in their 1875 catalogue, double the number of ten years earlier. Even so, right down to the end of the century there was no assumption in the Codes that a work of literature might be read in its entirety.

ALL'S WELL THAT ENDS WELL.

Stepmother (entering village school with whip). "MY BOY TELLS ME YOU BROKE YOUR CANE ACROSS HIS BACK YESTERDAY!"
Schoolmaster (turning pale). "WELL, I—I MAY HAVE STRUCK HARDER THAN I INTENDED, BUT——."
Stepmother. "I THOUGHT I'D MAKE YOU A PRESENT OF THIS WHIP. YOU'LL FIND IT'LL LAST LONGER AND DO HIM MORE GOOD!"

'Punch' provides much interesting comment on educational topics. Its viewpoint is generally biased, however, and a very patronising tone is often taken in the case of elementary schools. Jokes and cartoons usually depended for their humour on the speech patterns of working-class children, the philistinism of school managers and the low social position of teachers. This cartoon, dating from August 1901, hints that corporal punishment of the child was as much a feature of home life as it was of school life. The law required head teachers to keep a Punishment Book in which the name of the offender, the nature of the offence and the punishment given were to be recorded.

SCHOOL RECORDS

We can learn much about the functioning of Victorian elementary schools from the written records which were produced, especially log books, attendance registers, punishment books, and the reports of Her Majesty's Inspectors. Such records exist in considerable quantity from the middle years of the nineteenth century and will be found in the schools themselves, in local and county record offices and at the Public Record Office at Kew. Record-keeping was a sign of growing account-

ability, the need for which was as evident in the 1850s as it is today.

The grants to schools which the government introduced in 1846 proved almost impossible to control. In 1851 they stood at £150,000: by 1857 they had risen to £541,233. With the Crimean War having cost £78 million, it is not surprising that there were cries for retrenchment. In 1857 the Newcastle Commission was set up to consider ways of providing 'sound and cheap elementary instruction', and in

26

its report it found much that was wrong with the schools. One of the Commission's recommendations was 'payment by results', which the government introduced (though in a somewhat amended form) by the Revised Code of 1862.

Henceforth the government grant to a school was to be based on two factors only: attendance; and the results of an annual test of reading, writing and arithmetic to be conducted by a visiting Inspector. Children were to be grouped into

	Standard I	Standard II.	Standard III.	Standard IV.	Standard V.	Standard VI.
Reading*	To read a short paragraph from a book, not confined to words of one syllable.	To read with intelligence a short paragraph from an elementary reading book.	To read with intelligence a short paragraph from a more advanced reading book.	To read with intelligence a few lines of prose or poetry selected by the inspector.	Improved reading.	Reading with fluency and expression
Writing	Copy in manuscript character a line of print, on slates or in copy books, at choice of managers; and write from dictation a few common words.	A sentence from the same book, slowly read once, and then dictated. Copy books (large or half-text) to be shown.	A sentence slowly dictated once from the same book. Copy books to be shown (small hand, capital letters and figures).	Eight lines slowly dictated once from a reading book. Copy books to be shown (improved small hand).	Writing from memory the substance of a short story read out twice; spelling, grammar, and handwriting to be considered.	A short theme or letter; the composition, spelling, grammar, and handwriting to be considered.
Arithmetic†	Notation and numeration up to 1,000. Simple addition and subtraction of numbers of not more than four figures, and the multiplication table, to 6 times 12.	Notation and numeration up to 100,000. The four simple rules to short division (inclusive).	Notation and numeration up to 1,000,000. Long division and compound addition and subtraction (money),	Compound rules (money) and reduction (common weights and measures).+	Practice, bills of parcels, and simple proportion.	Proportion, vulgar and decimal fractions.

Notes:

*   'Reading will be tested in the ordinary class books, if approved by the Inspector; but these books must be of reasonable length and difficulty and unmarked. . .'

†   'The work of girls will be judged more leniently than that of boys. . .'

+   'The "weights and measures' taught in public elementary schools should be only such as are really useful; - such as Avoirdupois Weight, Long Measure, Liquid Measure, Time Table, Square and Cubical Measure, and any measure which is connected with the industrial occupations of the district.'

The Revised Code was itself revised on a number of occasions. This extract is from the New Code of 1879, by which date grammar, geography and history had been added as 'specific subjects', meaning that individual children rather than whole classes could be entered for the grant-awarding examination. Standards roughly corresponded to age. Six-year-old children were expected to reach Standard I. Standard VI was the expected level of an eleven-year-old child, although children were not compelled to stay at school to that age until 1893. The leaving age was raised to twelve in 1899. Although the curriculum for boys and girls was largely the same, there were many ways in which the 'hidden curriculum' discriminated against girls, as this table indicates.

Standards, covering the six years of school life. Standard I included children aged between six and seven; Standard VI those aged eleven to twelve. In 1882 a Standard VII was introduced. The curriculum for each standard was laid down, producing what was, in effect, a prototype National Curriculum. Minimum standards were prescribed, but the financial pressures on schools were so great that, in practice, these soon came to be seen as the peak of expectation.

The Revised Code has been criticised for its narrowness, but it had positive features, not the least being that the government was sending a clear signal to the voluntary schools that basic skills of literacy and numeracy were to be emphasised at the expense of religious teaching. In a sense, therefore, the Revised Code should be seen as a step on the way to the 1870 Education Act.

However, there can be no doubt that the annual visit by the Inspector could prove a traumatic experience, as so much depended on the outcome. Teachers, as well as children, were known to shed tears on such occasions.

The Revised Code required every head teacher to keep a log book, and these therefore become available for all inspected schools from 1863, although not all survive. The head teacher was required to copy into the log book the Inspector's report, and to sign it. This was no doubt a great humiliation whenever the report was unsatisfactory. The Code laid down that the head teacher should keep a 'bare record' of events in the school, and that 'no expressions of opinion' were to be entered. Fortunately for the historian this injunction was often ignored and, amongst the 'bare record' of admissions, attendance and visits by managers, we find the true voice of the teacher. For example, the head teacher of one school wrote in April 1864: 'Preparing for the New Code examinations is strange work, I believe it affects my nervous system, too many failures in Dictation or a sum makes me tremble, while a successful trial elates me perhaps beyond measure.'

The Revised Code at its most rigid lasted for only about fifteen years. From 1867 'specific subjects' such as history and geography started to qualify for grant, and gradually the curriculum was broadened out. By the 1890s many School Boards were grouping the oldest and ablest children into Higher Grade Schools offering a curriculum which, in some respects, resembled that of secondary schools. As School Boards were legally empowered to provide only elementary education, this extension of their role had its critics. In 1902 this criticism proved strong enough to sweep the Boards away and to replace them with Local Education Authorities, more within the mainstream of local government.

The voluntary societies had originally charged no fees but had commenced doing so by the 1830s on financial grounds, but also because it was claimed that payment strengthened parental responsibility and encouraged more regular attendance. This may have been true for those parents who received a regular and adequate wage, but it was certainly not true for all. Children were often kept away from school when the school fee could not be afforded, and general school attendance shot up when fees were eventually abolished. It was not the fee alone that was a burden, for the family also had to reckon on the loss of potential income from the child's own employment.

There was no 'standard' rate of elementary school fee, and variations existed both between regions and between providers. Roman Catholic schools (which often taught the poorest children) charged the lowest fees, while Anglican and Wesleyan schools charged the highest. Fees tended to reflect local wages. In south Staffordshire, a high-wage area, a fee of 4d a week was thought reasonable in the 1850s, but that would have been considered excessive in a low-paid agricultural area such as Dorset. At Haslingfield in Cambridgeshire in the 1840s fees were 1d for the children of labourers, 2d for the children of tradespeople, and 3d for those of farmers. Such a range was not untypical, and there were sometimes reduced fees when more than one child was sent to school.

28

The 1870 Education Act did not abolish fees, but it did lay down a maximum of 9d a week, a large sum which was nevertheless charged when the school boards came to establish 'higher grade schools'. In 1876 the Poor Law Guardians were empowered to pay school fees if application were made to them. However, many of them were reluctant to do so and remained unsympathetic. Virtually all elementary schools abolished fees in 1891, although it was not until 1918 that all such fees were finally abolished.

Log books are also full of information on reasons for poor attendance, and observations about bad weather and bad boots give a glimpse of the hard lives of the less well-off. Attendance was not made compulsory in 1870, although the question was hotly debated in Parliament. Issues such as parental responsibilities were raised, as well as the 'un-Englishness' of compulsion, but the simple fact is that there were not enough school places.

School attendance seriously concerned the Victorians, but there were differences of opinion between those who wanted children in school and those who wanted children at work. Child labour and school attendance were interlinked problems. The Factories Act of 1833 required all children between the ages of nine and thirteen who worked in textile mills to attend school for at least two hours each day. The law, however, proved difficult to enforce. In 1844 children working in mills were obliged to spend three whole days or six half days in school, thus commencing what was known as the 'half-time' system. Eventually the education provisions of factory legislation were extended to industries other than textiles, but children in agricultural employment remained unprotected until 1867, when the employment of children aged seven and under was prohibited.

The Agricultural Children Act of 1873 raised the minimum age to ten, but the law was difficult to enforce in rural areas, and children were frequently withdrawn from school, especially at harvest time, as attendance registers testify.

The 1870 Education Act empowered school boards, if they so chose, to frame by-laws to compel attendance, but many failed to do so. Ten years later, however, the framing of such by-laws became compulsory. Thereafter, all children in England and Wales were required to attend school until the age of ten, while children aged between ten and thirteen might leave once they had reached Standard Five. The 1880 Education Act had a significant impact on the number of children in school, for thereafter average attendance was in the region of 90 per cent. This was a dramatic turnaround, for twenty years previously children of almost 90 per cent of the population had *not* been in school.

After 1891, many of the remaining conflicts between the factory and the education laws were resolved, and in 1893 the school-leaving age was raised to eleven, which also became the minimum age at which a child could work in a factory. In 1899 the leaving age was raised to twelve.

Gradually, too, the state came to take on other responsibilities for the welfare of the young. After 1870 the great influx of children into schools brought to the public attention the extent to which many were malnourished and in poor health. In the 1890s anxiety grew over the alleged 'physical deterioration' of the nation, a concern made all the more grave by the number of men rejected, because they were unfit, for military service in the Boer War. Legislation in 1906 allowed local authorities to provide school meals (free in cases of need); and school medical inspection followed in 1907. From medical inspection it was but a short step to providing treatment.

Although much remained to be done, there can be no doubt that the Victorians made enormous strides in the provision of elementary education. They laid the foundation upon which twentieth-century educators might build. Their legacy was a solid one – as solid as bricks and mortar. In the early 1990s, half of all inner city first schools were built before 1900 and countless Victorian village schools still survive. Whatever their defects, it is hard not to feel some affection for the Victorian schoolroom.

FURTHER READING

Berry, George. *Discovering Schools*. Shire, 1970.
Burnett, John. *Destiny Obscure. Autobiographies of Childhood, Education and Family from the 1820s to the 1920s*. Allen Lane, 1982.
Digby, Anne, and Searby, Peter. *Children, School and Society in Nineteenth-Century England*. Macmillan, 1981.
Ellis, Alec. *Educating Our Masters. Influences on the Growth of Literacy in Victorian Working Class Children*. Gower, 1985.
Gardner, Phil. *The Lost Elementary Schools of Victorian England*. Croom Helm, 1984.
Goldstrom, J. M. *The Social Content of Education 1808-1870*. Irish University Press, 1972.
Gordon, Peter. *The Victorian School Manager*. Woburn Press, 1974.
Horn, Pamela. *The Victorian and Edwardian Schoolchild*. Alan Sutton, 1989.
Hurt, John. *Education in Evolution. Church, State, Society and Popular Education 1800-1870*. Paladin, 1972.
Hyndman, Michael. *Schools and Schooling in England and Wales. A Documentary History*. Harper & Row, 1978.
Landon, Joseph. *School Management*. Kegan Paul, 1883.
Lawson, John, and Silver, Harold. *A Social History of Education in England*. Methuen, 1973.
Lewis, June R. *The Village School*. Robert Hale, 1989.
Ringshall, Ron, *et al. The Urban School. Buildings for Education in London 1870-1980*. GLC and Architectural Press, 1983.
Seaborne, Malcolm. *The English School. Its Architecture and Organisation 1370-1870*. Routledge & Kegan Paul, 1971.
Seaborne, Malcolm. *Schools in Wales 1500-1900: A Social and Architectural History*. Gee & Son, 1992.
Seaborne, Malcolm, and Lowe, Roy. *The English School. Its Architecture and Organisation 1870-1970*. Routledge & Kegan Paul, 1977.
Sturt, Mary. *The Education of the People*. Routledge & Kegan Paul, 1967.
Sutherland, Gillian. *Elementary Education in the Nineteenth Century*. Historical Association, 1971.
Tropp, Asher. *The School Teachers*. Heinemann, 1957.

LOCAL STUDIES

There are many excellent local studies of Victorian education, including a number of 'archive packs' containing reproductions of nineteenth-century records. The following is only a brief selection.

Bushby, David (editor). *Bedfordshire Schoolchild. Elementary Education Before 1902*. Bedfordshire Historical Record Society, 1988.
Hurt, J. S. *Bringing Literacy to Rural England. The Hertfordshire Example*. Phillimore, 1972.
Johnson, Steve, and Leslie, Kim (editors). *Scholars and Slates. Sussex Schools in the 1880s*. West Sussex County Council, 1989.
Marsden, W. E. *Educating the Respectable. A Study of Fleet Road Board School, Hampstead, 1879-1903*. Woburn Press, 1991.
Sellman, Roger R. *Devon Village Schools in the Nineteenth Century*. David & Charles, 1967.
Silver, Pamela and Harold. *The Education of the Poor. The History of a National School 1824-1974*. Routledge, 1974.

PLACES TO VISIT

Intending visitors are advised to find out opening times and to check that relevant items are on display before travelling.

Beamish, The North of England Open Air Museum, Beamish, County Durham DH9 0RG. Telephone: 01207 231811. The museum buildings include a complete reconstructed board school of 1892, originally from the nearby village of East Stanley.

The Black Country Living Museum, Tipton Road, Dudley, West Midlands DY1 4SQ. Telephone: 0121-557 9643. St James's School (1842) has been rebuilt on the museum site.

Blists Hill Victorian Town, Legges Way, Madeley, Telford, Shropshire TF7 5DU. Telephone: 01952 586063 or 583003. A rebuilt Victorian school.

Bradford Industrial Museum and Horses at Work, Moorside Road, Eccleshill, Bradford, West Yorkshire BD2 3HP. Telephone: 01274 631756. A reconstructed schoolroom.

Braintree District Museum, Manor Street, Braintree, Essex CM7 3YG. Telephone: 01376 325266. A restored Victorian school.

Dewsbury Museum, Crow Nest Park, Heckmondwike Road, Dewsbury, West Yorkshire WF13 2SA. Telephone: 01924 325100. A reconstructed schoolroom, but of the 1940s.

Hitchin British Schools, 41/42 Queen's Street, Hitchin, Hertfordshire SG4 9TS. Telephone: 01462 452697. The Hitchin British Schools contain a Lancasterian schoolroom of 1837, together with other rooms added between then and 1905 and a rare galleried classroom of 1853 which is now restored as a working Victorian classroom. Also a schoolroom museum.

Katesgrove Schoolroom, Katesgrove Primary School, Dorothy Street, Reading, Berkshire RG1 2NL. Telephone: 01189 233268. This is a reconstructed schoolroom in a Board school built in 1873 and extended in 1891.

Leeds Industrial Museum, Armley Mill, Canal Road, Armley, Leeds LS12 2QF. Telephone: 0113-263 7861. Includes a reconstructed schoolroom based on an elementary school of the 1880s. Schoolroom not open to the general public.

Macclesfield Heritage Centre, Roe Street, Macclesfield, Cheshire SK11 6UT. Telephone: 01625 613210. The building was opened in 1814 as the Macclesfield Sunday School. The museum contains a reconstructed classroom.

Museum of Childhood, 42 High Street, Edinburgh EH1 1TG. Telephone: 0131-529 4142.

Museum of Childhood, Sudbury Hall, Sudbury, Ashbourne, Derbyshire DE6 5HT. Telephone: 01283 585305. The museum contains a reconstructed schoolroom.

Museum of Childhood, Judges' Lodgings, Church Street, Lancaster LA1 1YS. Telephone: 01524 32808. Room settings include a Victorian classroom.

Museum of the History of Education, Parkinson Court, The University, Leeds LS2 9JT. Telephone: 0113-233 4665.

Museum of Welsh Life, St Fagans, Cardiff CF5 6XB. Telephone: 01222 573500. A reconstructed school, and many artefacts relating to education in Wales.

Radstock, Midsomer Norton and District Museum, Barton Meade House, Haydon, Radstock, Bath, Somerset BA3 3QS. Telephone: 01761 437722.

Ragged School Museum, 46-50 Copperfield Road, Bow, London E3 4RR. Telephone: 0181-980 6405. The museum incorporates a recreated classroom in a building used as a Dr Barnardo's ragged school between 1880 and 1900.

St John's House (part of Warwickshire County Museum), St John's, Warwick CV34 4NF. Telephone: 01926 412021. The museum contains a reconstructed schoolroom.

Scotland Street School Museum of Education, 225 Scotland Street, Glasgow G5 8QB. Telephone: 0141-429 1202. The museum, which covers the history of education in

Scotland since 1872, is housed in a magnificent building designed in 1904 by Charles Rennie Mackintosh, the renowned architect, as an elementary school for the Glasgow School Board.

Sevenoaks Museum and Gallery, Sevenoaks Library, Buckhurst Lane, Sevenoaks, Kent TN13 1LQ. Telephone: 01732 453118 or 452384. A small schoolroom has been re-created here.

Sevington School, Sevington, Chippenham, Wiltshire SN14 7LD. Telephone: 01249 783070. Sevington School was built in 1848 and is now run as a museum by an educational trust.

Staffordshire County Museum, Shugborough, Milford, Stafford ST17 0XB. Telephone: 01889 881388 extension 211. The museum contains a reconstructed schoolroom.

The Museum of Local Life, Friar Street, Worcester WR1 2NA. Telephone: 01905 722349. Victorian classroom and plans for 1940s one.

Ulster Folk and Transport Museum, Cultra, Holywood, County Down, Northern Ireland BT18 0EU. Telephone: 01232 428428. The museum contains two schools re-erected from their original locations, Ballyveridagh National School, and Ballydown National School, both furnished as they would have been in 1900.

Weald and Downland Open Air Museum, Singleton, Chichester, West Sussex PO18 0EU. Telephone: 01243 811348. The museum has a reconstructed early nineteenth-century school from West Wittering.

Wigan Pier Heritage Centre, Wigan, Lancashire WN3 4EU. Telephone: 01942 323666. The museum contains a reconstructed schoolroom.

Worcestershire County Museum, Hartlebury Castle, Hartlebury, near Kidderminster, Worcestershire DY11 7XZ. Telephone: 01299 250416. Reconstructed early twentieth-century schoolroom.

The following museums are principally museums of childhood but contain some educational material:

Bethnal Green Museum of Childhood, Cambridge Heath Road, London E2 9PA. Telephone: 0181-983 5200.

Museum of Childhood, 1 Castle Street, Beaumaris, Anglesey LL58 8AP. Telephone: 01248 712498.

Many local history museums have displays associated with education and schooling.

Many Victorian schoolrooms remain in use to this day, either in working schools, or – as at the North of England Open Air Museum, Beamish – as classrooms where children studying history may enter into the spirit of the past. The Beamish school is a reconstruction of an 1892 board school, removed from the nearby village of East Stanley and reopened in its centenary year.